Contents

First published in November 1998 by the Audit Commission for Local Authorities and the National Health Service in England and Wales, 1 Vincent Square, London SW1P 2PN.

Printed in the UK for the Audit Commission Kent Litho.

ISBN 1 86240 075 X

Illustrations by Patrick MacAllister.

Introduction

Why has this paper been written?

1. Working in partnership with other organisations is a critical task for councils, police forces, health authorities and NHS trusts. The number of partnerships is growing, both in response to central requirements and as a result of local initiatives. Partnership working is a potentially powerful tool for tackling difficult policy and operational problems that local agencies face. It can also be a productive way of achieving more efficient and effective use of scarce resources.

2. Nevertheless, partnership working is difficult to do well and making partnerships work effectively is one of the toughest challenges facing public sector managers. Partnership working can also be costly, and partnerships can be justified only when their achievements outweigh the resources that they consume.

3. Although it is difficult to estimate the extent of partnership working precisely, both the numbers and scope of partnerships are increasing. This growth results from top-down and bottom-up pressures. Evidence of partnership working is already a pre-condition of access to important sources of funding, such as the Single Regeneration Budget (SRB) and the European Regional Development Fund (ERDF).

4. Mandatory partnership working is set to expand significantly as the Government implements its commitments to partnerships covering crime and disorder, health action zones, health improvement plans, youth offending teams, education action zones and early years development plans. Councils are likely to be given a duty to promote the economic, social and environmental well-being of their areas, which may lead to a further expansion of the partnership

approach. To help agencies to work together, the Government is also proposing to give councils and health bodies new powers to form partnerships, to commission services jointly and to pool budgets (Refs. 1 and 2).

5. The development of partnership working is generally to be welcomed. As many previous Commission studies have pointed out (Refs. 3, 4 and 5), the quality and cost effectiveness of services can be significantly improved when organisations work well together. Service-users recognise this [BOX A, overleaf]. The expansion of partnership working has also provided a means of ensuring that local agencies' work benefits from the expertise and ideas of the private and voluntary sectors.

...the quality and cost effectiveness of services can be significantly improved when organisations work well together.

BOX A

Citizens and business can see the difference successful partnerships make

The managing director of a research and development company comments on an economic regeneration partnership in the North West

'The partnership shows commitment to supporting business in the area. Being located in an inward investment centre, it provides a centre point for this activity within the area. It creates an infrastructure through which economic activity in the area is encouraged.

'We have recruited directly through the career service for the modern apprenticeships scheme … The career service has benefited from the partnership as it enables them to become more in touch with the kinds of skills that businesses require as we move into the 21st century. This obviously has advantages for the wider community in Wigan - matching skills with business needs creates a climate of growth.'

A tenant comments on a community development partnership

'The project has changed the atmosphere in the area. Schemes in the past were haphazard. The partnership works because different people work together; it pulls everyone in who all do their part and support each other. When someone promises something they have to come up with it; people have been let down in the past. The project has proved that it can bring services on to the estate with real benefits.

'The agencies are the key to working together. If you have a problem, you can pick up the phone and they will always listen. The partnership provides people with an opportunity to sit down with the agencies. It's not about what the agencies want but what the people want that's important.'

6. But, although there is little dispute as to the possible benefits of partnership working, these potential gains are often difficult to realise in practice. Many partnerships fail to achieve their full objectives, or are partnerships in name only. The track record of joint ventures in the private sector suggests that commercial partnerships also often fail to achieve their expected benefits, or do so only at a disproportionate cost (Ref. 6). Although some of the pitfalls facing commercial joint ventures and public sector partnerships differ, the high failure rate of commercial partnerships highlights the care needed in planning and implementing successful partnerships. The Commission's work on reorganisation in local government and the health service has also highlighted the difficulty of merging organisations (Ref. 7) and building effective joint working arrangements (Ref. 8).

7. As many previous Audit Commission publications (Refs. 3, 4 and 5) have shown, the reality is that joint working is beset by many obstacles. Occasionally these obstacles stem from national policies or requirements, which can:

- impose conflicting high-level objectives;

- restrict agencies' ability to pool resources and information;

- impose performance monitoring regimes that discourage collaboration;

- limit the powers available to agencies to address problems; and

- distort locally identified needs and priorities.

...the time and effort required to run the growing number of partnerships is considerable...

8. There are even more local obstacles, most of which result from the inherent difficulties of getting a range of agencies with differing purposes, structures and ways of doing things to work together. Common difficulties in partnership working include:

- getting partners to agree on priorities for action;

- keeping partners actively involved;

- preventing the partnership from becoming simply a talking shop;

- making decisions that all partners endorse;

- deciding who will provide the resources needed to achieve the partnerships objectives;

- linking the partnership's work with partners' mainstream activities and budgets;

- monitoring the partnerships effectiveness;

- working out whether what is achieved justifies the costs involved; and

- avoiding 'partnership overload', particularly where agencies are each involved in large numbers of partnerships.

9. Partnership working is often expensive, as well as difficult. Many of the costs involved, particularly senior and middle managers' time, are not routinely recorded and few partnerships have precise information about the costs of their activities. Nevertheless, it is clear that the time and effort required to run the growing number of partnerships is considerable: larger authorities might now participate in as many as 50 separate arrangements with other public agencies or with the private and voluntary sectors.

10. If partnership working is to provide good value for money, it is essential that these costs are outweighed by the benefits achieved. It is worrying, therefore, that few partnerships have collected the sort of information that would tell them whether this is the case.

About this paper

11. The paper follows the main stages in the lifecycle of a partnership, spelling out the likely problems and some ways of overcoming them. It covers:

- deciding to go into partnership;
- getting started;
- operating efficiently and effectively;
- reviewing the partnership's success; and
- what partnerships can expect to achieve.

12. Each section ends with a set of key questions which are drawn together in the centre of the paper in a pull-out checklist. Individual agencies may find this helpful in reviewing their involvement in partnerships or assessing the potential value of new partnerships under consideration. Partnerships may wish to use the checklist as a starting point for reviewing their activities.

13. We have used the term 'partnership' to describe a joint working arrangement where the partners:

- are otherwise independent bodies;

- agree to co-operate to achieve a common goal;
- create a new organisational structure or process to achieve this goal, separate from their own organisations;
- plan and implement a jointly agreed programme, often with joint staff or resources;
- share relevant information; and
- pool risks and rewards.

14. The paper does not specifically address contractual arrangements between public and private sector bodies (including Private Finance Initiative projects) (Ref. 9) for delivery of services. Although such contractual arrangements are sometimes referred to as partnerships, they differ from the partnerships considered here because they stem from mutually compatible rather than shared objectives. However, contractual arrangements can have partnership characteristics (Ref. 10), and much of the good practice described in this paper could benefit organisations in their commercial contractual relationships.

For whom has this paper been written?

15. This paper aims to help board and authority members and senior officers in local government, the NHS and the police to make better decisions about when to set up a partnership and to improve the effectiveness of existing and future partnerships. Others contemplating or already involved in partnerships - including voluntary and private sector organisations - may also find it helpful. The paper may be of interest to central government departments.

The evidence on which this paper is based

16. The paper is based on fieldwork in 14 different partnerships and the experiences of over 150 people. These partnerships are mostly well established and cover a range of different activities. The Commission was helped by an advisory group which acted as a sounding board throughout the preparation of the paper. However, the conclusions are those of the Commission alone.

1. Deciding to go into partnership

17. Although partnership working is increasingly common, it does not necessarily follow that a partnership is the answer to any problem. Agencies should consider carefully what they hope to achieve before setting up a new partnership and whether there are other, simpler ways of realising their objectives. This section looks at:

- why organisations develop partnerships; and

- when a partnership may not be the best approach.

Why work in partnerships?

18. There are five main reasons why agencies develop partnerships:

- to deliver co-ordinated packages of services to individuals;

- to tackle so-called 'wicked issues';

- to reduce the impact of organisational fragmentation and minimise the impact of any perverse incentives that result from it;

- to bid for, or gain access to, new resources; and

- to meet a statutory requirement.

Delivering co-ordinated packages of services

19. In recent years, there has been a growing awareness of the importance of focusing on the user's experience of public services. This frequently means that agencies must work together both to deliver packages of services that are tailored to individual users' needs and to plan co-ordinated service strategies that enable such packages to be delivered in practice. Although the principles underlying this kind of collaboration are simple, it is often difficult to achieve in practice.[1]

Although partnership working is increasingly common, it does not necessarily follow that a partnership is the answer to any problem.

20. Nevertheless, well-planned partnerships are one of the best mechanisms for improving the quality and co-ordination of services, particularly to vulnerable individuals whose needs might otherwise be neglected. This kind of provision can be particularly important if vulnerable people are only a small proportion of all service-users, because the needs of small groups of users can easily, if inadvertently, be marginalised.

---

[1] Several of the Commission's recent publications (Refs. 3, 4, & 5) illustrate the extent and consequences of poor collaboration in practice.

...the needs of small groups of users can easily, if inadvertently, be marginalised.

21. Offenders with mental health problems who have been released from prison are a good example of this type of service-user. If their needs are not anticipated and met, the consequences both for individual prisoners and for the wider community can be extremely serious. However, only a minority of prisoners have mental health problems, and they are a very small minority of health service users. So, although their needs are very important in themselves, they are rarely at the core of either the prison or health services' operational priorities. A partnership approach to planning and delivering services can reduce the risk of such people falling through the safety net [CASE STUDY 1].

CASE STUDY 1

Improving services that are provided by a range of agencies

The Wessex Project was started in 1993 by local social services, the probation service, prison service and NHS. The needs of offenders with mental health problems had not previously been the top priority for any of the agencies involved in the project. Its aim was to make sure that offenders with mental health problems started using the community-based services that they needed as soon as they were released from prison. To ensure that the partnership could influence both policy and operations, it included a steering group of senior managers as well as a project team of staff who had been seconded from the different agencies.

In the early stages of the project, the participating agencies found it difficult to respond in a co-ordinated way to individuals' needs because they viewed these needs too narrowly - from their own particular professional agency perspective. The project helped to improve planning of services for individuals. It also revealed that a hitherto relatively neglected group of people was larger and more significant than individual practitioners had assumed: during the project, about one-quarter of people in prison and one-third of those on remand were found to have a history of mental health problems.

After three years, the project had broken down the barriers to interagency working and shown how agencies could co-ordinate care. Those responsible for specific services no longer feel threatened by other agencies' involvement, networks to exchange information have been developed, and partnership approaches to working have become routine. Having achieved its aim and brought interagency co-ordination into the mainstream of each partner's approach to delivering services, the formal partnership structure was no longer considered necessary and was therefore dissolved.

Tackling 'wicked issues'

22. Local agencies – particularly councils - are increasingly concerned with complex problems, such as community safety or economic regeneration, which cross traditional organisational boundaries [EXHIBIT 1]. A clearer recognition of the major concerns of communities and changes in national policy have given increasing prominence to these so-called 'wicked issues'. These issues present some extremely tricky challenges that agencies cannot hope to tackle adequately unless they work together. Councils frequently play a key part in partnerships of this type. The proposed new duty for councils to promote the economic, social and environmental well-being of their areas (Ref. 2) recognises this special community leadership role, and may serve to encourage the establishment of further partnerships.

EXHIBIT 1

'Wicked issues'

Problems facing agencies cross traditional professional boundaries.

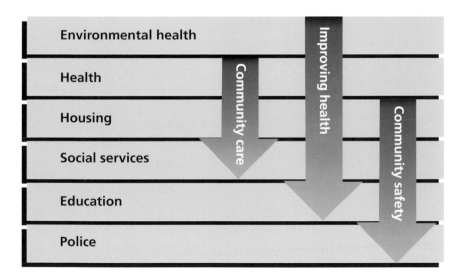

Source: Audit Commission

Reducing the impact of organisational fragmentation

23. These shifts in local and national agendas have coincided with the increasing fragmentation of local service delivery. A number of new agencies have been set up, some existing agencies have been separated into purchasing and providing arms and others have been given greater autonomy from their parent bodies. New agencies have sometimes been set up to tackle newly identified problems but, more frequently, they take on tasks previously carried out by others. As the number of organisations working on different aspects of a service increases, the importance of collaboration between them grows.

Bidding for new resources

24. Many partnerships are set up to enable agencies to bid for resources, such as the SRB, which are not available to single organisations. As the role of challenge-type funding expands, this sort of partnership is becoming increasingly common. The fate of such bid-led partnerships has been mixed.

25. In principle, a partnership should be an effective way of ensuring that such special funds are well used, and there has been some good practice. However, setting up a partnership simply to bid for money carries particular risks, particularly where one organisation is especially keen to secure the resources and recruits partners mainly to enable it to do so. When a partnership is set up on this basis, there is an increased risk that the instigating partner will be particularly dominant, with other partners initially lacking a real stake in or commitment to the arrangement. To address this, agencies setting up a bidding partnership need both to convince potential partners that signing up will be of benefit to them and to allow each partner to make a real contribution to the project.

Meeting a statutory requirement

26. Although there are powerful reasons why agencies opt to work in partnership, there are circumstances in which they have little or no choice but to do so. While the growing number of challenge-type funds run at national or European level, which are accessible only to partnerships, do not compel agencies to work in partnership, they provide a real incentive for them to do so. The number of such challenge initiatives is expanding: education and health action zones are recent examples.

27. Meanwhile, the Government is increasingly giving local agencies statutory duties to work together. Community safety, early years education and health improvement are three areas where partnership approaches are, or will shortly be, obligatory. The concept of a duty for one agency to work with another is not new: joint consultative committees between health and social services authorities have been in existence since 1977. Nevertheless, the scale of statutory partnership working is set to expand rapidly.

28. This expansion will pose special challenges for some agencies. A vital ingredient in successful partnership working is the commitment and enthusiasm of the partners. Where a problem is a good candidate for partnership working but local agencies have not adopted this approach voluntarily, there may be questions about their ability to work successfully together and to secure the benefits that agencies in other areas have achieved. When this is the case, agencies need to ask themselves what the obstacles to partnership have been in the past and to work out how to overcome them in future.

29. Agencies should treat the arrival of these new statutory duties as an opportunity rather than an imposition. Government can encourage local agencies to rise to the challenge by providing appropriate assistance and incentives (Refs. 1 and 2). But, ultimately, the onus is on local agencies to respond positively to the challenge to secure the benefits for their communities that successful partnerships can bring.

When not to work in partnership

30. Because partnership working can be both difficult and expensive, it is essential that organisations consider other options as well as a partnership. Depending on the circumstances, a different approach could be either more efficient, more effective, or both.

31. Other options include:

- consultative arrangements, where a single agency retains responsibility for decisions and actions;

- networks of personal or professional relationships which do not have to involve organisational commitment; and

- contractual relationships, such as those established under the Private Finance Initiative, which produce different benefits for the different partners.

32. Projects can, of course, move between different models of co-operation during their existence, using a formal partnership model only when this is essential.

33. Agencies should also ask themselves whether they have, or can develop, the capacity to run a successful partnership [BOX B]. The main ingredients are described in detail in later sections of this paper.

BOX B

Questions to ask before setting up a partnership

- Is the problem that the prospective partners want to solve one that needs a partnership approach?

- Do the prospective partners have a clear and shared vision of the benefits that the partnership is intended to achieve?

- Is this vision realistic in the light of:
  - the resources and opportunities likely to be open to the proposed partnership?
  - the issues that partnership working is particularly suited to address?

- Will the anticipated benefits outweigh the likely costs (direct and indirect) of a partnership?

- How will the costs and benefits be measured?

- Could the benefits be achieved in a simpler or more cost-effective way?

- Are the partners all willing to devote the necessary time and effort to make the partnership succeed?

- Do the partners all know what role they will play, what resources they will contribute and how they will account for the success of the project?

- Are the partners willing to consider changing their other activities to fit in with the partnership's objectives, where this is appropriate?

Factors indicating that a partnership is not the best approach

- The answer to one or more of the questions above is 'no';

- The topic proposed is primarily the responsibility of one agency, with others having only a marginal interest or role;

- Agencies have no shared objective in relation to this topic;

- Agencies' main aim is to achieve cost savings;

- Agencies have a history of poor relationships and have not made a commitment to change this; and

- Agencies want to shunt costs or blame for problems on to one another – that is, there is a hidden negative agenda.

DECIDING TO GO INTO PARTNERSHIP
QUESTIONS FOR AUDITED BODIES AND PARTNERSHIPS

1 Does this organisation have clear and sound reasons for being involved in its current partnerships?

2 Where new partnerships must be set up to meet national requirements, what groundwork is being done locally to maximise their chances of success?

3 Are changes in behaviour or in decision-making processes needed to avoid setting up partnerships with only limited chances of success?

2. Getting started

34. Partnership is a slippery concept that is difficult to define precisely. A distinction can be made between setting up a partnership entity or process (formal partnership) and a style of working where organisations behave to one another as partners regardless of the formal links between them (informal partnership). Informal partnership arrangements are especially hard to define, particularly if there has never been a formal, explicit, partnership in operation and individuals do not see themselves as being involved in partnership working.

35. This paper is primarily concerned with formal partnerships, although the behaviours that characterise informal partnership working are an essential component of successful formal arrangements. The rest of this section looks at:

- common partnership functions;
- major current topics of formal partnership working;
- the main models of formal partnerships;
- an essential structural requirement for all partnerships; and
- choosing the right partners.

Functions for partnerships

36. Partnerships usually carry out one of the following functions:

- to develop a vision for a community - which could be a locality or a group of people with similar needs - and monitor progress towards it;
- to formulate medium- or long-term strategic objectives to turn a shared vision into reality;
- to plan the actions necessary to meet agreed strategic objectives; and
- to carry out joint operations, which could include major capital projects, new services to individuals or new approaches to existing services.

37. Although partnerships can operate at all four levels, they should usually aim to focus on only one or two at any one time: trying to do too much at once will almost certainly result in partners feeling overwhelmed and losing commitment to the arrangement. However, over a number of years a single partnership may carry out all of these functions in turn. When this happens, the partnership will need to change to reflect its developing role. New partners may be needed when moving from the planning to an operational phase; representation, structure and legal status may all also need to be reviewed.

Topics for formal partnerships

38. Not surprisingly, in view of the reasons why partnerships are set up (see paragraphs 18-29), the most common areas for formal partnership working have been services that need to be delivered seamlessly across organisational boundaries, and policy problems that no single agency can address alone.

39. The most common current partnership topics include:

- economic and/or social regeneration;
- crime prevention;
- community safety;
- environmental improvement;
- improving public health; and
- developing long-term strategies for the development of a geographical area.

The main models for partnership arrangements

40. Partnerships vary enormously in both size and scope. At one end of the spectrum, large strategic partnerships can involve up to 100 members and address the major issues of a big city. At the other, a smaller community-based partnership can deal with the problems of a single estate. Given their varying size and scope, it is perhaps not surprising to find that there is no common model for successful formal partnerships. In fact, there are four main models, each with advantages and disadvantages.

Separate organisation

41. In this model the partners set up a distinct organisation with a separate legal identity from that of the individual partners. It is most suitable for larger partnerships with a medium- or long-term lifespan and for those which need to employ staff and oversee large programmes of activity. The main advantages of creating a separate organisation are:

- a clear, strong identity for the partnership;
- a separate identity that can give the partnership credibility with external organisations, which is greater than that of the individual partners;
- a separate body may be able to do things that the individual partners cannot;

- dedicated partnership staff who can identify readily with the separate organisation;

- a reduced risk that one partner will dominate; and

- although creating a separate entity can involve resolving complex legal and financial questions, addressing these questions helps to clarify liabilities and responsibilities within the partnership.

42. The main disadvantages are:

- the formal commitments that partners need to make when forming a separate entity may be off-putting for partners from small community organisations, who may be unused to this way of working; and

- the partner organisations may become distanced from the partnership, particularly if it takes on too much of a life of its own, and has an agenda that is driven by its employees rather than its board of partners.

'Virtual' organisation

43. In this model, the partners give the partnership a separate identity, but without creating a distinct legal identity. The partnership may look independent, with its own name, logo and premises, and staff who see themselves as answerable to the partnership rather than to an individual partner. However, at a formal level, one partner employs any staff and manages resources. This model has the advantage of avoiding some of the tricky issues that need to be addressed when setting up a legally separate entity while keeping the advantages of a distinctive partnership identity. However, this model, and the other less formal arrangements outlined below, may leave responsibility and accountability within the partnership unclear. In addition, the partner which employs the staff and manages the resources can end up dominating the partnership.

Co-locating staff from partner organisations

44. This is a less formal model, where a group of staff from the partner organisations work together to a common agenda, usually under the aegis of a steering group. Sometimes the partners will pool resources to support the partnership's work, but any staff continue to be managed separately by the partner which employs them. The main difference between this and the virtual organisation model is that, in the former, staff see themselves as, say, police officers who happen to be working on a community safety project, but in the latter they see themselves as community safety partnership workers who happen to be police officers.

45. This model is particularly suitable for partnerships that do not need to present a strong separate identity to the outside world. It can work well if partners trust one another sufficiently to feel comfortable with a relatively informal arrangement. However, it is less suitable than the more formal options for managing major new projects and it can lead to confused loyalties for staff.

Steering group without dedicated staff resources

46. This is the simplest and least formal model. The partnership consists simply of a steering group without either dedicated staff or budget, so its outputs must be capable of being implemented through partners' mainstream programmes and staff. This is an ideal model for a partnership that aims to improve the co-ordination of day-to-day service delivery across organisational boundaries, although it is unlikely to be effective unless steering group members have sufficient authority to ensure that mainstream practices can be changed. It is less suitable for partnerships that need a long lifespan to achieve their objectives, or a separate identity either to galvanise partners into action or to attain external credibility.

An essential structural requirement for all models

47. Diversity of structures makes good practical sense, but every partnership has certain basic requirements. Every partnership needs at least one body - a board or steering group – which all the partners recognise as the partnership's mechanism for making decisions. A properly structured partnership board is essential to make sure that the partnership delivers its objectives and remains accountable to the partners. However, its composition is not an easy matter, especially where a large number of organisations are involved. This difficulty is not just about numbers: different types of organisation - such as large businesses or local community

groups - have ways of working which are often difficult to combine.

48. One solution to the problem of board size in large partnerships is to create a smaller executive committee with a selection of key partners, which does not attempt to be fully representative. The full partnership can then play a more deliberative role: addressing key issues without deciding on the

operational detail, receiving information and monitoring progress. In some partnerships this committee focuses on strategy while the wider group concentrates on operational matters. In others, the roles are reversed [CASE STUDY 2]. Any executive must operate openly in order to avoid becoming a clique or making other partners feel they are being excluded from important decisions.

CASE STUDY 2

Executive structures

For its first three years, **Kirklees Health for All** had a steering group comprising mainly middle managers from the health authority, local trusts, voluntary sector groups and the council. There was good team working on the ground, but the partnership had little influence over the planning processes in the partner organisations. In 1995, a new four-level structure was established:

- a joint executive team made up of the health authority's and health trust's chief executives and an executive director of the council, providing a framework for strategic direction and priority-setting;

- a commissioning group, looking at the overall planning of services, that comprised senior officers and voluntary sector representatives;

- action groups for each of the main target groups, focusing on more detailed service planning, with a 'health for all forum' of community representatives to inform and monitor their work; and

- a project team for each interagency project.

Choosing partners

Identifying the right organisations

49.   In areas where partnership working is either mandatory or a pre-condition of a bid for resources, the choice of core partners may be determined partly in advance: police forces and councils must work together on community safety partnerships, for example. Even if there is no requirement to include particular organisations in a partnership, the choice of core partners may be obvious. This is particularly the case where the partnership's main objective is to improve the co-ordination of service delivery and it must therefore embrace all those involved in delivering the service. However, even in areas where some partners are self-selecting, there are still choices to be made about:

- who else to involve beyond the core partners (should the private sector be involved in an education action zone partnership, for example, and if so, are local businesses the right partners or should the private sector's contribution also include suppliers of educational services); and

- which organisations from within a sector or interest group to bring on board (should all local businesses be invited to join a regeneration partnership, for example, or only those that employ significant numbers of local people, or both?)

50.   There is no blueprint for deciding the right number of partners or whom to bring on board. Partnerships that are trying to take a strategic approach to a complex problem may need a large number of members in order to encompass all the key players in a sizeable geographical area. Similarly, partnerships that aim to generate a wide-ranging vision for the future of an area will need to involve large numbers of organisations if community interests are to be fully represented. Partnerships concerned with co-ordinating existing activities are often smaller, but should still consider carefully how to ensure that service-users' views are brought into the partnership's work.

Identifying the right individuals

51.   Getting a new partnership off the ground usually takes flair, drive and determination. Therefore, in the early days of a partnership the most important factor to consider in identifying the right individuals to involve is whether they have the leadership qualities necessary to convince other potential partners to participate, to persuade external stakeholders to commit resources and to generate a persuasive vision of what the partnership could achieve. In short, new partnerships need champions with the charisma, authority and negotiating skills to get the show on the road. These champions are often not the right people to lead the partnership throughout its life, but they have a vital galvanising role in the early days.

...new partnerships need champions with the charisma, authority and negotiating skills to get the show on the road.

GETTING STARTED
QUESTIONS FOR AUDITED BODIES

4 Have all the partnerships in which the organisation is involved been reviewed to evaluate whether the form of the partnership is appropriate to its functions and objectives?

5 Do all the partnerships have an appropriately structured board or other decision-making forum?

6 When setting up a new partnership, how are prospective partners identified?

52. Putting a partnership together and starting work can take a lot of time and effort. However, this will be wasted if the partnership cannot then find ways to operate efficiently and effectively. The next section looks at some of the commonest day-to-day pitfalls of partnership working and how to avoid them.

3. Operating efficiently and effectively

53. Although partnerships can be very effective, they face a host of potential pitfalls. Some of these are the day-to-day difficulties of co-ordinating large numbers of organisations with differing responsibilities, outlooks and ways of doing things. In addition, because partnerships are often trying to find solutions to complex, even intractable, problems, it is all too easy for good ideas to fail to deliver in practice. This section considers:

- how to maintain partners' commitment and involvement;

- getting things done;

- making good use of partnership staff;

- building trust between partners;

- keeping a focus on outcomes; and

- linking the partnership's work to partners' mainstream activities.

Maintaining commitment and involvement

54. A partnership can be effective only if all the partners are appropriately involved in its work. That does not mean that they should expect to make identical or equivalent contributions: a grass-roots community organisation will not usually be able to offer the financial or staff resources that a police force or health trust can bring, but may be able to contribute valuable information and contacts that no other agency can offer. However, unless all partners believe that they are meaningfully involved in the partnership's work, those who feel on the margins will become disengaged. If this happens, the potential benefits of partnership will be difficult to achieve.

55. Maintaining active involvement, particularly of a large number of partners, is time-consuming. Strategic partnerships need significant input from councillors, board members and senior managers, whose time is scarce and costly. Operational partnerships take up the time of specialists who could be adding value in other ways. Time spent in formal partnership meetings is only the tip of the iceberg. Far more significant is the time needed to understand the other partners, to manage the complex set of relationships and to act on the partnership's decisions. The need to keep all the partners on board can lead to slow and complex decision-making structures, where the partnership moves at the pace of the slowest members.

56. In the early stages of a partnership, slow decision-making may be inevitable, particularly if the partnership is large or there is a legacy of distrust between agencies. However, mature partnerships where trust has been established should consider:

- delegating lead responsibility for particular projects to individual partners; and

- nominating a group of partners to act as an executive.

57. If a small group of partners acts as an executive, all partners should satisfy themselves that they have the legal powers to agree to such a process. They should also consider how they can avoid a situation in which a few partners, particularly those who are largest and best resourced, dominate entirely. Options include rotating executive responsibility between different partners or having an executive that is made up of partners from different sectors.

Getting things done

58. If partnerships are to be more than interesting talking-shops, they must find effective means of making decisions and taking actions that further their objectives.

Making decisions

59. The means by which a partnership makes decisions depends on the type of structure that it has adopted (see paragraphs 40-46), although most partnerships operate on the basis that major decisions cannot be made unless all partners support them. Partnerships commonly experience some difficulty in coming to decisions. This can simply be because partners cannot readily reach agreement on the way forward, and take time to find a suitable compromise.

60. A partnership's work can be seriously impeded if prospective decisions all have to be separately ratified by the partners in advance, and if the partners' decision-making processes or timetables do not fit well together. The easiest way round this problem is to make sure that the members of the partnership's board have sufficient authority to commit their organisations to a particular course of action. Partnerships should also plan their work carefully so that they know well in advance when decisions with significant policy or financial implications will need to be made. It is vital that all partners have sufficient time to evaluate the implications of major prospective decisions and to consider their own legal and financial advice.

61. When the partnership's timetable is externally driven (by the deadline for submitting a bid for resources, for example), the partners should identify and consider the main choices available to them at the outset of their work. Good project planning can ensure that all the partners' agreement is secured in time.

62. Partners must also find ways of co-ordinating the work of the multi-agency arrangements in which they participate with their own planning and decision-making processes. There are two risks here. The first is that no real link is made between the partnership's activities and those of its members. If this happens, it will be difficult for the partnership to bring about the changes that it needs but cannot deliver itself, a particular problem for partnerships that are dealing with service co-ordination or strategic planning. Weak links between the partnership and its partners' planning processes will also limit what the partners can learn from the partnership's work.

63. The second risk is that partners set up new mechanisms to track partnerships' work, rather than feeding it into those that exist, or reforming these if necessary. This can result in additional bureaucracy that adds little value. For example, one council that had been successful in bidding for SRB money set up a series of new subcommittees of councillors that mirrored each of the SRB partnership boards. These created extra meetings for hard-pressed councillors but did not succeed in linking the SRB projects' work to the authority's forum for considering its regeneration strategy.

64. Another common problem is that partners find themselves involved in lengthy debates about who will provide the resources needed to implement decisions. These issues may need to be thoroughly addressed, particularly if in the past partners have adopted practices that have increased pressure on one another's budgets (so-called 'cost shunting') (Refs. 4 and 5). However, it does not make sense for partners to spend a lot of time debating who will pay for small items of expenditure.

Taking action

65. There are two main ways in which partnerships can make sure that their decisions are followed up by action: either they can have their own dedicated staff (sometimes called 'single agency action'), or partners' representatives on the board/steering group can take responsibility for ensuring that decisions are turned into action ('multi-agency action').

66. Both approaches have pros and cons. If a partnership can rely on dedicated staff to implement decisions, it is more likely that action will indeed be taken. Using dedicated staff is also a constructive way of preventing senior staff from the partners, who may be involved in significant numbers of partnerships, from becoming over-burdened by the work that they generate. However, dedicated partnership staff may struggle to bring about lasting change in partners' mainstream activities or in their ways of thinking.

Making good use of partnership staff

67.   Effective partnerships are characterised by their ability to see solutions where others might find only intractable problems. This requires a flexible approach and an openness to new ways of thinking. Such an approach makes particular demands of partnership staff, whether they are employed full-time by the partnership, are secondees or are involved for only part of their time in the partnership's work. The staff of a community safety partnership, for example, must be able to understand the way that all the partners approach this issue now, but must also be able to think 'outside the box' to develop new approaches to the problem. If

some partners are entrenched in approaches that are not working, partnership staff need to be able to cajole them into seeing the need to change without alienating them.

68.   Partnership staff need to be familiar with the partner organisations and have a wide range of contacts within them. They also need to understand the organisational context of those

with whom they will work. Some partnerships publish information about the management structures, policy priorities and other features of the partners. Information of this kind is valuable, but it is no substitute for direct experience. This is why some partnerships deliberately employ staff with experience of a range of different organisations [CASE STUDY 3].

CASE STUDY 3

Employing the right staff

The Thames Valley Partnership is made up of councils, the police, other justice agencies and private firms. The Partnership, which is concerned with community safety, uses secondments extensively. Some secondees work full-time for a limited period, while others work some of the time for their employing organisation. Full-time staff are encouraged to keep in touch with their organisations. The partnership is keen that both the partnership and the secondee will benefit from the experience, so wherever possible the chief executive of the partnership is involved in staff selection. In this way, the partnership draws on a wide range of skills from private and public sector backgrounds. It constructs teams to take advantage of different but complementary working styles.

Watford Borough Council is involved in many partnerships. Recognising partnership work as a core part of its role, the council has recently carried out an internal reorganisation to enable it to optimise its involvement in partnerships. It sees having the right staff as a vital part of creating a good partner organisation and has therefore appointed senior staff with private and voluntary sector experience to ensure good liaison with other partners and to give an insight into working styles in other kinds of organisation.

Building trust between partners

69. For most partnerships, building trust between partners is the most important ingredient in success. This may be particularly difficult if the problem that the partnership is addressing stems from a legacy of mistrust or conflict between different agencies. It also takes time. One large urban regeneration partnership holds regular 'awaydays' for partners to have a frank exchange of views on the partnership's progress. These help to develop trust by encouraging partners to understand their policy differences more fully, but they do represent a substantial investment of time. However, a high level of trust within the partnership is one of the best ways of avoiding the risk of excessive bureaucracy that can arise when partners feel that they must all be involved in every detail of the partnership's operations.

70. Although it is essential that partners trust one another, they must be wary of what one partnership chief executive called 'the dangers of collusion' – that is, the risk that partners will be so preoccupied with maintaining good relationships with one another that they lose sight of their external objectives. One way of minimising this risk is for partnerships to expose their performance to external challenge. This could be done by regular testing of users' satisfaction with their progress and activities. Another route is to keep referring back to the partership's objectives to ensure that it stays on track.

Keeping a focus on outcomes

71. Partnerships should also make sure that their working style strikes a good balance between developing the partnership itself and focusing on hard-edged objectives and the extent to which these are achieved. It is surprisingly easy for partnerships to lose sight of their overall objectives in a flurry of activity or to assume that implicit objectives or a shared desire to work together are enough [CASE STUDY 4]. Partnership objectives should be consistent with those of the partner organisations, and partners' representatives need to know where the boundaries lie between the partnership's work and their own organisation's activities.

...building trust between partners is the most important ingredient of success.

CASE STUDY 4

Setting objectives

Health for Huntingdonshire was established because the partners recognised the need to work together, but no clear objectives were set at the outset. The wide-ranging composition of the steering group, including some groups with a very local focus, led to confusion about the level at which the partnership should operate. There were also concerns that some localities were getting preferential treatment.

The partnership has now reduced the steering group to four core partners. It has drawn up a statement of purpose, responsibilities and core value. This clarifies Health for Huntingdonshire's role as a strategic partnership, working towards the broad aim of better public health. More detailed objectives are being drawn up.

Action plans have also been produced for some of the local projects to realise the partnership's aims. For each plan, the aims, action required, timescale, responsibilities and reporting requirements have been clearly defined and progress is being monitored.

...the long-term impact of a partnership which is sustained by one charismatic individual is usually limited.

Linking the partnership's work with partners' mainstream activities and budgets

72.   One of the most common reasons for setting up a partnership is to strengthen service delivery, particularly of cross-cutting services, where partners recognise either that existing arrangements are not meeting users' needs effectively or that services focus on reacting to problems rather than preventing them. In short, partnerships are frequently seeking better ways of doing things. While a special arrangement like partnership may be a good way of harnessing the efforts needed to find the right solution to such problems, these solutions will be effective in the longer term only if they are adopted into the day-to-day practice of the partners.

73.   An earlier section of this paper discussed the important role which 'partnership champions' often play in the early life of a partnership arrangement. The early enthusiasm and determination of such individuals can be critical. Nevertheless, the long-term impact of a partnership which is sustained by one charismatic individual is usually limited. The partnership champion may move on to another project, but even if he/she does not, the skills needed to see the partnership through the delivery phase of its work are usually rather different from those that are needed to bring the partners together at the outset. But, most importantly, it is rarely possible for one person to bring about the changes in organisational behaviour that many partnerships need to achieve their objectives.

74. The key measure of success for many partnerships is the extent to which they bring about changes in the way that partners behave in terms of:

- partners' policies; and/or
- operational service-delivery arrangements; and/or
- decisions about allocating resources.

75. A beneficial shift in attitude or behaviour can sometimes be achieved relatively easily, by partners recognising the impact which their actions have on one another's work, or by seizing an opportunity to make links between policies which had not previously been seen as connected. For example, public health partnerships with local authorities have encouraged health bodies to recognise the multiplicity of factors that affect health in a locality. By the same token, councils are examining the health implications of policies that were not previously considered to have a health dimension – for example, transport.

76. But influencing the partners' mainstream behaviour in this way can also be difficult, for both logistical and policy reasons. Partnerships are often grappling with problems that are embedded in 'vicious circles', and it can be difficult both to identify how to break out of the circle and to take the critical first steps.[I] Other barriers to achieving change in partners' mainstream behaviour include:

- policymakers' reluctance to adopt innovative new approaches which may carry a level of risk;[II]
- the sheer complexity of getting a number of large organisations to agree on a common change of direction, particularly where different decision-making processes or cycles make getting agreement a cumbersome process; and
- organisational inertia – the 'but we've always done it this way' syndrome.

The key measure of success for many partnerships is the extent to which they bring about changes in the way that partners behave...

[I] In some policy areas where agencies often find themselves in such vicious circles (for example, providing long-term care for older people), local obstacles to breaking out of the circle can be inadvertently reinforced by national policies or processes that tend to encourage reactive rather than preventive services.

[II] This reluctance can be a particular problem if the changes being proposed are seen by those outside the partnership as resulting mainly from the partisan enthusiasm of individuals who champion the partnership.

77. These barriers to change can be lowered by:

- careful planning of the actions needed to secure the necessary agreement to change;

- persuading stakeholders outside or on the edge of the partnership's active membership of the case for change (by involving them in devising solutions, or in joint training, for example);

- testing new service-delivery models in pilot projects; and

- devising mechanisms to equalise the organisational gains and losses that can sometimes result from breaking out of a vicious circle.[I]

78. The greater mutual understanding and respect that result from successful partnerships can also play a vital role in encouraging organisations to consider changes in their approach

---

I   This cannot always be achieved at a local level: The Commission's report, *Coming of Age,* for example, recommended national consideration of changes to funding arrangements to help agencies to adopt practices that support elderly people living at home.

or spending priorities that they might otherwise not have been prepared to consider [CASE STUDY 5].

79. Partnership working is often exciting for the participants: many of those involved see it as one of the more stimulating and rewarding parts of their job. As partnerships become an established part of the public sector scenery, it would be easy for them to be seen automatically as a 'good thing'. But even if a partnership overcomes all the day-to-day obstacles to effective operation, it must still demonstrate that it adds value. The next section looks at how partnerships should evaluate their work.

CASE STUDY 5

Changing partners' priorities

The improved working relationship between Coventry City Council and West Midlands Police that has developed through their joint work in the **Coventry Community Action Against Crime** partnership has led both agencies to review how they allocate their core budgets (the partnership itself is mainly funded through the SRB). The police have now appointed a full-time liaison officer, based in the council headquarters, to each of the seven local authorities in their area.

In turn, the City Council has allocated funds to the 'Reclaiming Coventry' initiative, which will spend £540,000 over two years on a four-pronged approach to improving community safety. The programme covers:

- law enforcement;

- domestic security;

- social support, such as victim support; and

- preventative measures.

This approach has led to reductions in recorded crime of 17 per cent and 24 per cent in two pilot areas. It is now being extended.

OPERATING EFFICIENTLY AND EFFECTIVELY
QUESTIONS FOR AUDITED BODIES AND PARTNERSHIPS

7   Do partners share the same main objectives for the partnership?

8   Are the partnership's objectives consistent with those of the partner organisations?

9   If an outsider watched a partnership operate, would he/she be able to identify the partnership's main objectives?

10   Do the partners know where the boundaries between the activities of the partnership and of their own organisations lie?

11   Do the members of partnership steering groups have sufficient authority to commit their organisations to decisions?

12   Are partnerships prepared to delegate responsibility for parts of their work to particular partners?

13   Do large partnerships have an executive group that all the partners trust to make decisions on their behalf?

14   Are project-planning techniques used to ensure the separate agreement of all the partners to a course of action in good time, when necessary?

15   Do the partnership's decisions get implemented effectively?

16   Are partnership staff selected for their technical competence and for their ability to operate both inside and outside a conventional public sector framework?

17   What actions are taken to build and maintain trust between partners?

18   If members have dropped out of a partnership, what lessons have been learnt about how to maintain involvement in the future?

4. Reviewing success

80. This section looks at the actions that partnerships need to take to evaluate whether their work is having its intended impact and to ensure that they are accountable both to their 'owners' (the partner organisations) and to their 'stakeholders' (those who are intended to benefit from the partnerships work). It covers:

- measuring progress;
- testing value for money;
- ensuring accountability; and
- planning the end of the partnership.

Measuring progress

81. Although it is a challenging task, partnerships must look for ways of measuring their success if they are to justify a continued existence. There is no blueprint for evaluation beyond the requirement that it relates clearly to the partnership's objectives. Some partnerships, particularly those that are set up to bid for resources, must measure progress against criteria set by funders. These criteria are – quite legitimately – concerned with the funder's national or regional objectives. However, most partnerships find such imposed measures of limited value for their own local purposes and they must therefore devise their own framework for measuring progress.

82. It is frequently difficult to evaluate the extent to which a partnership has succeeded. Some measurable outcomes, such as reductions in morbidity levels, crime or unemployment, emerge only over the long term and interim progress may be difficult to measure except by indirect means.

83. Even where a partnership has relatively easily measurable objectives (such as a reduction in certain sorts of crime), it is hard for partnerships to determine how far any changes are attributable to their work. Nevertheless, there are good local and national reasons for measuring such outcomes. Such monitoring can shed some light on the impact that partnerships may be having and, if most partnerships with similar objectives are using similar measures, it may be possible for them to compare their relative effectiveness and learn from one another.

84. In other cases, measuring performance can be difficult because the necessary information is either unavailable or not systematically and consistently collected. Data collected by one agency may need to be matched with data held by another to get a complete picture of the partnership's impact, but the definitions that agencies use and the populations covered by their data often differ. These disparities can make it difficult for partnerships to track the impact of their work coherently. Wherever possible, partnerships should design relevant data collection into their activities from the outset.

85. Despite these difficulties, all partnerships should plan to devote time to designing a review framework that covers both the outcomes of the partnership's work and the health of the partnership itself.

Outcomes

86. The first step is for partners to identify the main objectives that the partnership is intended to achieve. Partners should then turn these objectives into specific outcomes – that is, answer the question, 'How will I know when these objectives have been achieved?' The next step is to identify which of these outcomes can be measured by numerical performance indicators. These may include factors that the partnership's members control directly as well as those that they want to influence but which are also affected by others. A basket of indicators is usually needed (paragraph 89 and BOX C give more guidance on setting partnership performance indicators). Partners should then identify the best ways of assessing whether goals that cannot be measured numerically have been achieved. This may involve surveys of users; setting up focus groups or user panels; using information from complaints or feedback systems; observing the partnership's influence over non-members; or a formal evaluation study by an external agency.

The partnership and its processes

87. Partnerships should also measure:

- the efficiency of their activities (the principles here are those that apply in any single agency); and

- the health of the partnership itself – that is, how well the partners are working together.

88. Partnerships should avoid spending too much time looking at how well the partners are interacting: the point of forming a partnership is to improve performance, and this should principally be measured through the eyes of service users, citizens and other stakeholders. However, improved performance in areas that benefit from partnership working is strongly influenced by the quality of the working relationships between the partners. Reviewing these relationships is critical if the partnership is having difficulty in keeping the commitment and involvement of some members. Valuable ways of doing this include using checklists to identify how well partners think relationships within the partnership are working; having a standard agenda item on how the partnership is working; and using awaydays for review. Partnerships that identify substantial problems with the internal health of the partnership should consider asking an external facilitator to help to resolve them.

Using performance indicators

89. One of the best ways of measuring the impact of a partnership is to devise performance indicators that measure the impact of its work. The majority of existing national performance indicators address the work of individual agencies, but partnerships need to set performance measures that look at the effect of multi-agency interventions. It is critical that these measures are owned by all the partners: if the partnership's work is measured through indicators that only some partners can influence, the others may feel marginalised or those whose work is being measured may feel that the whole burden of making the partnership succeed is falling on them (Ref. 11). There are several steps involved in setting up good systems of cross-cutting performance indicators [BOX C].

BOX C

Setting cross-cutting performance indicators

There are two main types of cross-cutting indicators:

* those which relate to problems where agencies must work together to be effective but where each agency's performance can be measured discretely (for example, the time a social services authority takes to assess the social care needs of someone leaving hospital); and

* those where a number of agencies' activities have an impact on the outcome being measured (for example, crime rates).

Because individual partners are currently subject to different regulatory or performance measurement regimes (or none), there can be incentives to act in ways that do not help to resolve the cross-cutting problem. The performance of individual schools, for example, is monitored by published league tables of exam and test results, which may give schools an incentive to exclude difficult pupils. When pupils are excluded, their risk of getting involved in crime increases. A partnership looking at juvenile crime therefore needs to set targets and monitor performance concerning school exclusions and levels of juvenile crime.

Some agencies are more used than others to preparing performance information and to reporting or discussing it in public. Agencies that are unused to these activities would face quite a steep learning curve. This can be addressed by the more experienced partners providing support and assistance, but the learning required is not just about raising levels of technical expertise. There may be organisational culture obstacles to overcome as well.

...the point of forming a partnership is to improve performance, and this should principally be measured through the eyes of service-users, citizens and other stakeholders.

90. Despite the difficulties that partnerships face in evaluating their impact, they are none the less more likely to make some attempt to measure their success than the partners are when acting separately. Although funders' performance-measurement requirements are often seen as burdensome, they do help to foster a culture of evaluation and review [CASE STUDY 6]. Academic interest in partnership working can also be turned to advantage; partnerships can sometimes gain funding to support detailed external research into their effectiveness, the results of which can be fed into their future practice.

Testing value for money

91. All partnerships should evaluate whether they are on course to achieve both their immediate and long-term objectives, and most need to build further on their current arrangements for doing so. However, even when a partnership has a comprehensive evaluation framework, this in itself is not enough. The key test is whether the extra benefits that come from working in partnership are greater than the costs involved in doing so.

CASE STUDY 6

Measuring success

One of **Birmingham City Pride's** first tasks was to draw up a prospectus setting out its vision for the city and its strategic objectives under six headings:

- economy;
- regional capital (including transport);
- environment and housing;
- social conditions;
- young people; and
- community regeneration.

The prospectus set out a range of performance indicators under each heading to demonstrate over the partnerships ten-year life how well its objectives had been achieved. For each indicator, a benchmark showed the 1995 position (where available) and the target for 2005. The partnership has published two annual reports, for 1995/96 and 1996/97. In the latest, the partnership has amended and improved some of the indicators, dropping some that were proving too difficult to measure. The partnership is committed to using performance indicators, and other European cities are starting to emulate its work.

The costs of partnership

92. The specific costs arising from partnership working will depend on the scale and structure of the partnership. Where it is responsible for activities that are additional to those of the partners, and employs or seconds staff to manage these activities, the costs will usually be significantly greater than those of partnerships which are improving the co-ordination of existing activities. However, in most cases, partnerships have both direct and opportunity costs.

93. The main opportunity cost is the time spent by partnership board members in meetings and that which both board members and others invest in the partnership's work between formal meetings. Although these opportunity costs are rarely quantified, they are just as real as direct costs and should be considered in the same way. The main opportunity cost for a large local authority involved in a wide range of partnerships is a significant proportion of some senior officers' time: many chief executives report spending up to half their time on involvement in partnerships.

94. Few partnerships monitor the costs of their activities systematically. Those which are legally independent entities tend to have a clearer idea of the costs of their activities because they must publish accounts but, even then, many do not count the indirect costs of their activities. The costs of operating some typical partnerships (including time spent in meetings but excluding time spent progressing work between meetings other than by partnership staff) can be estimated [**EXHIBIT 2**].

EXHIBIT 2

Partnership costs

The direct and opportunity costs of operating partnerships are not always monitored, but they can be estimated.

Type, scale and cost of partnerships

£8,000-£10,000	£70,000	£150,000
SMALL Aiming to improve co-ordination of existing activities	**MEDIUM-CRIME PREVENTION** A programme of separately funded activities	**LARGE CITY STRATEGY** Overseeing a programme of separately funded activities

Two members within the partnership

Source: Audit Commission

Weighing costs and achievements

95. Relatively few partnerships make full estimates of the costs of their work (including indirect or opportunity costs), so few are in a position to weigh these costs against their achievements. This tendency is worrying. If partnerships do not review both the costs and achievements of their work, they will not be in a position to demonstrate that they are delivering good value for money. As partnership working expands, it will be vital for partnerships to make better arrangements both for tracking the value of the resources that they use and to satisfy themselves and others that they are generating good value.

The costs of not working in partnership

96. Although it is essential that partnerships monitor the costs of their existence and can demonstrate that these are outweighed by their achievements, it is important also to bear in mind that significant costs can be incurred when organisations fail to work as partners. These costs are sometimes difficult to measure: they might, for example, be the distress and inconvenience that

users suffer when services are poorly co-ordinated, or the opportunities that local people miss out on when local economic development is weak. Partnerships can also generate in kind contributions to their work (for example, free use of privately owned conference accommodation or free advertising space), which might not be available to the individual partners.

Being accountable

97. One of the main benefits of partnership working can be a better alignment of services with users' needs. Individual service-users may therefore experience partnerships as more responsive to their needs than are their constituent partners. However, in legal, political or financial terms, partnerships are often less clearly accountable than their individual members. This can make it difficult for individual service-users to seek redress if things go wrong. It also raises important questions about the corporate governance of partnerships.

98. Partnerships need to decide how they can make sure that their activities are accountable :

- to the members of the partnership;

- to stakeholders outside the partnership, including funding bodies; and

- to service-users and the public at large.

Accountability within the partnership

99. Maintaining accountability within the partnership should present problems only for large partnerships where all partners do not have the same level of day-to-day input. When only a minority of members represents the others, the risk is that either the leading partners carry the burden of consulting the others, or that some partners feel less involved and lose commitment as a result. Some partnerships overcome these problems [CASE STUDY 7] by:

- using annual general meetings or planning days involving all partners;

- circulating information or soliciting views via computer networks; and

- careful agenda planning so that the board can canvass the views of other members in advance.

CASE STUDY 7

Reinforcing accountability to partners

Thames Valley Partnership includes 18 local authorities alongside the police, other justice services and many private sector representatives. There is a board of 15, representing only a cross-section of partners. Each of the partners has different interests, so no single channel of communication is appropriate. Instead, the partnership uses:

- top-level contacts between the partnership's chief executive and those of the partner organisations;

- feedback to their parent organisations by secondees;

- a well-attended annual meeting;

- regular seminars and conferences; and

- topic-based forums for managers and practitioners.

Wigan Borough Partnership prepares a quarterly report for all the members of the borough council. Members can monitor the partnership's activity and the involvement of their representatives on the partnership board - the leader, chief executive and chair of the economic resources committee.

The partnership prepares separate reports for the City Challenge forums. These enable community groups not directly represented on the partnership to influence its work.

...in legal, political or financial terms, partnerships are often less clearly accountable than their individual members.

Accountability to other organisations

100. Other partnership stakeholders include funders, Government or interest groups that could be affected by the partnership's decisions. Funders usually make their feedback requirements clear. But there can still be problems if different funders are asking for large amounts of different performance data to be captured. Organisations outside the partnership can also be adversely affected by its activities [CASE STUDY 8]. Some partnerships tackle this risk by including new members, setting up consultation mechanisms with affected groups or carrying out risk assessment to determine the likely effects of their activities.

CASE STUDY 8

Reinforcing accountability to stakeholders

A borough council set up a partnership with traders in its town centre after they complained that it was slow to respond to their views and suggestions for improvement. The partnership set up a fast-track mechanism to feed traders' views into the council's decision-making process. This successfully resolved the original problem, but does not take account of the views of other groups with an interest in developing the town centre.

Making partnerships accountable to the public

The **Healthy Croydon Partnership** has set up and funded a community empowerment project, managed by the voluntary sector, to ensure that members of the community can be actively engaged in the Parternship's work.

The staff of the partners involved in a service improvement/regeneration project covering the **Bell Farm** estate in York:

- hold regular surgeries in the estate office when residents are encouraged to comment on the quality and range of services partners provided as well as raising specific problems; and

- visit residents at home to tell them about the partnership's services and to gather their views.

Birmingham City Pride holds partnership meetings in public and circulates details of discussions and decisions to organisations outside the partnership.

Accountability to service-users and the public

101. Maintaining accountability to the general public or to service users is a challenge for partnerships, especially those that do not involve representative community organisations. The most successful partnerships hold themselves to account, creating an atmosphere in which the partners challenge each other, regularly revisit the partnerships original purpose and communicate extensively with local people [CASE STUDY 9].

Corporate governance

102. The way in which a partnership can be held formally to account for its activities or use of resources depends on its structure. If the partnership has independent company status, it will appoint its own auditors, and board members will be expected to act in the best interests of the company rather than in those of other organisations that appointed them to the board. In this situation, the mechanisms by which a member of the public could expect to hold a mainstream public body to account (for example, public rights to see council or police authority reports or to attend meetings) are not readily available. However, a partnership which has independent company status may still have clearer corporate governance arrangements than a less formally structured partnership.

103. The regulatory regimes that apply to public bodies (and can offer reassurance to the public about how public money is used) do not apply in full to all the partnerships in which those bodies participate. Even where one partner acts as the lead agency, managing resources or employing staff, and there is a greater level of public reassurance, it may still be unclear – both to individual citizens and to other organisations - who is really responsible for making sure that public money is being used properly and effectively. Where a partnership is externally funded, the reporting requirements, often imposed by the funding body, do not necessarily allow scrutiny by the general public.

104. As partnership working expands, the 'fit' between existing regulatory regimes and cross-organisational working arrangements will require attention. Consideration also needs to be given to whether partnerships involving public bodies should be required to meet in public and to give the public rights of access to information. In the meantime, every partnership should consider:

- holding some or all of its meetings in public;
- regularly publishing information about its activities and finances; and
- reviewing its own corporate governance arrangements.

105. If they have not already done so, councils, police forces and health bodies should consider how to bring their involvement in partnership work within their corporate governance arrangements, particularly internal and external audit work on financial probity and value for money.

Planning a partnership's end

106. There are positive and negative reasons why formal partnerships come to an end. Partnership working is often experimental and innovative projects may fail. Partnerships sometimes find that their task is being done better elsewhere or that their objectives cannot be achieved at a reasonable cost. Individual partners' strategies and circumstances can change so that the partnership's objectives are no longer a priority.

107. However, closing a formal partnership can be a positive measure of success. If the partnership's main objective was to see through a major capital project, then the completion of the project will usually herald the end of the partnership, at least in its original form. Similarly, where the aim was to co-ordinate services properly, the formal partnership can be replaced by informal partnership approaches to day-to-day activity once the appropriate mechanisms are up and running [CASE STUDY 1, p10].

...the 'fit' between existing regulatory regimes and cross-organisational working arrangements will require attention.

108. Whether the end of a partnership is a sign of success or failure, forward-thinking organisations should plan in advance for its end. Every partnership therefore needs either:

- an exit strategy, which allows the partnership to be discontinued and plans alternative means of maintaining the gains that have been achieved; or

- a continuation strategy, where exit is not appropriate.

109. In the heat of setting up a new partnership, it is not easy to envisage its end. But doing so helps to focus more sharply on what the partnership can realistically achieve [**CASE STUDY 10**]. Thinking early about how the partnership's work will be sustained in the future can also help to avoid leaving a legacy of problems, particularly financial commitments that others will need to pick up.

CASE STUDY 10

Reviewing direction

Croydon Health Authority and **Croydon Borough Council** set up 30 projects in 1995 to reduce the gap between the health of residents in the two poorest areas of the borough and the rest of the population. The two authorities committed £1 million a year over three years, partly from joint finances but mainly from their core resources.

Both parties considered exit and sustainability strategies from the start. Each project is reviewed quarterly, with a major review after two years, to consider:

- whether the project should continue beyond the three-year funding horizon;

- whether it should be incorporated in a wider 'Healthy Croydon' initiative; and

- what changes, if any, are needed to the project's timetable or objectives.

The review results are presented regularly to both the funding agencies.

REVIEWING SUCCESS
QUESTIONS FOR AUDITED BODIES AND PARTNERSHIPS

19 Does each partnership have a shared understanding of the outcomes that it expects to achieve, both in the short and longer term?

20 What means have been identified for measuring the partnership's progress towards expected outcomes and the health of the partnership itself?

21 Has the partnership identified its own performance indicators and set jointly agreed targets for these?

22 Are the costs of the partnership known, including indirect and opportunity costs?

23 Are these costs actively monitored and weighed against the benefits that the partnership delivers?

24 What steps have been taken to make sure that partnerships are accountable to the individual partners, external stakeholders, service users and the public at large?

25 Are some or all of the partnership's meetings open to the public?

26 Is information about the partnership's spending, activities and results available to the public?

27 Does the partnership review its corporate governance arrangements?

28 Has the partnership considered when its work is likely to be complete, and how it will end/hand over its work when this point is reached?

5. What can successful partnerships expect to achieve?

110. So far, this paper has concentrated on the difficulties that organisations encounter in setting up, running and monitoring effective partnerships. But although partnership working is challenging, and more partnerships fail than succeed, successful partnerships can achieve goals that individual agencies cannot. This section looks at four areas where partnership working has demonstrated its potential value:

- aligning the services provided by the partners with the needs of users;

- making better use of resources;

- stimulating more creative approaches to problems; and

- influencing the behaviour of the partners or of third parties in ways that none of the partners acting alone could achieve.

Aligning services more closely with users' needs

111. The services that public sector bodies deliver reflect their statutory functions and are normally within a prescribed and specialised range. But, increasingly, the social issues of most concern to the public - fear of crime, poor environment, unemployment or drug abuse –can best be tackled by partnerships, which either develop long-term strategies or aim to provide a seamless service to specific customers [CASE STUDIES 1 and 11].

CASE STUDY 11

Realigning services with needs

Birmingham City Pride brings together all the agencies in the city that can improve the quality of life for its citizens. The City Council is a major player. The City Pride Board also includes senior representatives from business, the voluntary sector, community groups, Birmingham university, the health authority and the police.

City Pride has no executive authority. The agencies remain independent and individually accountable. But participants report that City Pride helps to focus attention on the important cross-boundary issues by subjecting different agencies' plans to peer scrutiny and by setting performance indicators.

This approach has helped to make City Pride's partners' own planning processes more robust. In some cases it has also improved communication between different departments of large organisations.

Wigan Borough Partnership incorporates the Chamber of Commerce, Training and Enterprise Council (TEC), Careers Service and the economic development functions of the Council. Under TEC rules, the board has a private sector majority, but the borough council is represented by its leader, chief executive and chair of the economic resources committee.

The partnership is a key player in debates about the future of the area and had significant input into the Council's regeneration strategy - Fulcrum 2000. But its main focus is on implementing that strategy by providing a one-stop service to local business, prospective investors and the borough's existing and potential workforce. The partnership now employs 230 staff.

The partnership is organised into six directorates, which cut across the old organisational boundaries and focus instead on the needs of those who use their services.

Making better use of resources

112. Partnership working can improve the effectiveness with which resources are used by:

- using joint planning to deploy resources more effectively;

- making use of spare capacity; and

- sharing information.

113. A joint planning framework can sit anywhere on a spectrum from a vision statement of the partners' aspirations to the means for developing detailed operational plans. But the key point is that it prompts partners to identify how pooling their skills and resources can achieve maximum effect [CASE STUDY 12].

114. Partnerships can also make good use of spare capacity, especially under-used buildings. For example, partner agencies can use community or company-owned premises as a base for services that may attract target groups which might be reluctant to use services based in council or health authority premises [CASE STUDY 13].

CASE STUDY 12

Effective joint planning

Coventry Community Action Against Crime is a partnership between Coventry City Council, West Midlands Police and 14 other public, private and voluntary sector agencies. Three years of joint working have improved the relationship between the Council and the police in particular which has, in turn, resulted in cross-agency strategic and operational plans. This partnership has also resulted in area action plans that combine higher levels of visible police activity with improvements to the security of flats and houses, closed-circuit TV surveillance, public awareness campaigns about crime prevention and the targeting of advisory services such as victim support.

CASE STUDY 13

Making use of spare capacity

Groundwork Merthyr & Rhondda Cynon Taff has been working with 14 other agencies to regenerate a council housing estate in the centre of Merthyr Tydfil. The estate suffered from a spiral of decline; its reputation discouraged people from moving there and properties that were left empty were then vandalised, further depressing the estate's reputation. The partnership, which includes Merthyr Tydfil Council, Safer Merthyr Tydfil and the NSPCC, has developed empty council properties into new residents' facilities, including a family centre which runs after-school activities, parents' groups and training courses for local volunteers. Nearby, three formerly empty buildings are now a furniture recycling and skills centre, and a block of empty properties has been earmarked for development into a supported housing complex, lifeskills centre and GP clinic.

115. Information is usually an under-used resource, both within and between organisations. An open approach to sharing information distinguishes effective partnerships from some other types of joint-working relationships - especially contractual ones. Although contractual relationships can encourage their participants to improve the precision of the information that they produce and monitor, they can also discourage the most open form of information-sharing. One of the most common benefits that results from partnerships is that newly available information can enable partners to target their mainstream activities more effectively. There are some necessary restrictions on the exchange of information about individuals, but also much scope for information previously held in different places to be combined to good effect [CASE STUDY 14].

CASE STUDY 14

Sharing information

The Healthy Batley project – part of the **Kirklees Health for All** partnership has been trying to identify new ways of improving the health of groups with a high incidence of health problems. Batley has a large Asian community, and its members are strongly represented in local licensed taxi driving businesses. This community has a higher than average incidence of diabetes - a significant health problem for the individuals afflicted, but also a risk for passengers and other road-users if symptoms are not adequately controlled. The Council's taxi-licensing department is now involved in a co-ordinated strategy to promote better health within this group of people.

...newly available information can enable partners to target their mainstream activities more effectively.

Stimulating more creative approaches to problems

116. Partnerships' ability to find new solutions to policy and operational problems is one of the greatest potential strengths of this way of working. Innovation can result from the simple step of bringing together people with different backgrounds, skills and assumptions. A problem that has defeated the determined efforts of one organisation may be solved if others take a fresh look at it, or if groups that are seen as the source of a problem - such as young people - are given a say in what should happen [CASE STUDY 15]. Using partnerships' ability to find creative approaches to problems is particularly valuable if the problem being addressed is lodged in a 'vicious circle'.

CASE STUDY 15

New solutions to old problems

Restormel Crime Prevention and Community Safety Partnership is a partnership between Restormel Borough Council, Cornwall County Council, Devon and Cornwall Police, the Rural Development Commission and Cornwall & Isles of Scilly Health Authority. There is also private sector involvement. Its initial aim has been to reduce the risk of offending by young people in the area around St Austell, a problem that was previously seen only as a policing issue.

The partnership has found new ways to tackle juvenile crime. During the summer of 1996, there was a large increase in the number of incidents of disorder and criminal damage thought to have been committed by young people. The local police station was overwhelmed with public complaints and demands for action, but the police felt dissatisfied with the results of their attempts to engage with the local community. The partnership's full-time officer and youth service representative arranged a public meeting for young people to voice their views on the underlying causes of local youth crime. Senior representatives of the relevant agencies attended and a plan of action was drawn up. This helped to reduce youth dissatisfaction while also reassuring the adult population that their concerns were being addressed.

During the summer of 1997, the number of incidents of disorder and criminal damage involving young people dropped by around half, releasing significant police resources for other work.

117. Partnerships can encourage experimentation and thus generate innovative service improvements [CASE STUDY 16]. Such improvements might happen without a formal partnership, but good partnerships involve trust and the sharing of risks and rewards, both of which make innovation more likely.

...good partnerships involve trust and the sharing of risks and rewards, both of which make innovation more likely.

CASE STUDY 16

Innovation in services

The Healthy Batley project - part of the **Kirklees Health for All partnership** - found that women of Asian ethnic origin had high levels of coronary heart disease and took little organised regular exercise. The partnership brought together the Council's baths management and health and fitness teams with community groups and health promotion staff to work out how to provide activities that would appeal to this group. As a result, men are excluded from the baths for one afternoon a week and women can swim while dressed. Asian women who did not take exercise before are now regular participants.

Influencing others

118. Partnerships frequently wield greater influence than their individual partners. In many cases, the impact of a partnership on third parties comes from having a distinct identity. Firms that might otherwise be reluctant to contribute to a local authority programme of environmental improvement in which they have little say, might be persuaded to do so by an independent agency in which business has a role [CASE STUDY 17].

...the impact of a partnership on third parties comes from having a distinct identity.

CASE STUDY 17

Changing behaviour

The **New Leaf** partnership started from an initiative by Brent Council to involve local businesses in the environmental issues facing the borough. The partnership now includes the Council, local businesses and residents' and community groups. The partnership has been influential in three areas:

- persuading local property-owners to carry out environmental improvements (helped by match-funding from City Challenge and the SRB);

- providing practical advice to firms, community groups and schools on improving their environment by, for example, reducing waste; and

- raising environmental awareness through public events and newsletters.

New Leaf has been able to stimulate involvement in a wide range of events including an annual Environment Week and the Brent Green Awards.

The Council believes that it could not have achieved these results single-handed.

Gurnos Regeneration Partnership

This estate regeneration project was underpinned by a Safer Cities crime prevention programme. Since Groundwork Merthyr & Rhondda Cynon Taff and Safer Cities started operating on the estate, burglary rates have reduced by 46 per cent after one year and 69 per cent after two; and the fear of crime has dropped by 50 per cent. South Wales Police says that the partnership has had a clear impact on the public's attitude towards its officers. The local community has started to ask for police surgeries so that they can work together against crime, and they report that complaints about the police are becoming progressively more minor.

6. Conclusion

119. Partnership working is well established in the public sector and there is some evidence that it is bringing real benefits. Partnerships can improve public services by generating solutions to problems that single agencies cannot solve, improving the co-ordination of services across organisational boundaries and making better use of existing resources. Partnerships can also exert greater influence than their individual members could achieve. They could, therefore, potentially play a powerful role in local community governance, bringing together those who can best act as advocates for a range of interests.

120. However, these benefits have a cost. Working in partnership takes more time than working alone; partnerships require specific skills from both individuals and organisations; considerable effort is usually needed to make a partnership arrangement work satisfactorily; and evaluating the results may take years. Although partnerships can make services more responsive to individual users, they can make lines of political and financial accountability less clear than when agencies work alone.

121. The key ingredients for a successful partnership are:

- clear, shared objectives;

- a realistic plan and timetable for reaching these objectives;

- commitment from the partners to take the partnership's work into account within their mainstream activities;

- a clear framework of responsibilities and accountability;

- a high level of trust between partners; and

- realistic ways of measuring the partnership's achievements.

Partnership working is well established in the public sector and ... it is bringing real benefits.

122. Many of the techniques and practices that help successful partnerships to deliver are straightforward: there is no great mystery about them. But although they are common-sense, they are by no means common practice. It is surprising how few partnerships know the full costs of their activities, for example, or can evaluate their achievements in the light of their costs. If partnership working continues to expand, it is essential that such basic good practice is more widely implemented.

Many of the … practices that help successful partnerships to deliver are straightforward…